# SATURDAY MORNING TEA

The Power of Story
to Change Everything

## By Tony Bridwell

Author of *The Maker* Series

# SATURDAY MORNING TEA

## The Power of Story
## to Change Everything

# By Tony Bridwell

Author of *The Maker* Series

To my daughter, Alli Koch, aka, Sis.

# The
# INTRODUCTION

"I didn't have time to write a short letter,
so I wrote a long one instead."

Mark Twain

This quote has been credited to Mark Twain, borrowed from a letter he wrote in 1871. Supposedly, Twain once received this telegram from a publisher:

"NEED 2-PAGE SHORT STORY TWO DAYS."

He responded:

"NO CAN DO 2 PAGES TWO DAYS. CAN DO 30 PAGES 2 DAYS. NEED 30 DAYS TO DO 2 PAGES."

Writing with brevity poses a unique and interesting challenge. In the words of Thomas Jefferson, "The most valuable of all talents is that of never using two words when one will do." For that reason, this is a different type of book for me. Not only did I limit the story to two main characters, but I also trimmed half the words to accommodate a short plane ride, a couple of morning commutes, or maybe an early morning cup of tea. This story—written about the power of story—is meant to be enjoyed in one or two sittings.

Our lives are part of a greater story. In her book, *Wired for Story*, Lisa Cron wrote, "Story is the language of experience."

Personally, professionally, even organizationally, we embody a collection of experiences which are the starting point for how we navigate life. Experiences form the skeletal system of our self-worth and shape our engagement with culture. Our experiences impact how we think and feel, which in turn motivates what we do. Simply put, experiences are the fuel of life. What is the chemical formula of this fuel? Story!

To fully unpack the power of story could fill volumes. After all, psychologists have been deliberately unpacking the inner workings of the mind for centuries. While it is impossible to fully exhaust the rich mines of research, many of the gems have woven into the fabric of this short story.

The diary of King Solomon has preserved this timeless wisdom: 'There is nothing new under the sun." However, we have uncovered new insights to help solve the mysteries of not only *who* we are but *how* we are.

Along with Solomon, I believe we are all here for a higher purpose. I see our individual journeys as part of a much bigger—often unseen—story.

Do I struggle in my journey? Every day. But that doesn't mean I am a victim of meaningless circumstances. Viktor Frankl wrote, "Everything can be taken from a man but one thing: the last of human freedoms—to choose one's attitude in any given set of circumstances, to choose one's own way."

My story—with every trial and triumph—matters, as does yours. The purpose of this book is to provide a glimpse of what fuels life, to give insight into some of the workings of our days and offer comfort as we identify the circumstances we can and cannot control.

The backdrop of the story is personal for me in many ways. For the past 15 years, my daughter, Alli (a.k.a. "Sis"), and I have enjoyed a Saturday morning breakfast together. Two years ago, our morning tradition became a live Saturday podcast that now includes guests who join us for breakfast and share their stories.

For more than a decade, Alli and I have stumbled through hundreds of conversations about life. In retrospect, it is easy to observe how the stories we have shared continue to shape our story today. The podcast has become a way to preserve those stories for the future and to share them with as many who care to listen.

Finally, early in my career—as a first-time manager of people—I made a lifetime quota of mistakes with those I led. Most—if not all— have mixed emotions about the past. Part of me would enjoy a do-over, but I also recognize that those skinned-knee moments crafted, for better or worse, the person I am today. If there is any regret, it is in the misery I created for those in my path during my younger years.

It is because of the struggle early in my career that I've deliberately set the scene for my fifth book around a first-time leader of people. If there is a story I could tell my younger self, it would be this one. This is part of the story I've been telling my daughter over Saturday morning tea.

By speaking my story with my daughter, I have learned that I still have the ability to learn. The journey continues, and there are choices to make each day. The good news is, it is never too late to change *the* story. The harder part is condensing it into just the right amount of words.

# The
# PROFESSOR

"Never assume everyone knows what you know
at the level you know."

The knot in Leah's stomach tightened as she surveyed the packed tea shop. She was juggling a scone in one hand and a hot cup of tea in the other. Her computer bag dangled off her shoulder, the weight reminding her of the dire mission at hand. The cup and saucer rattled, threatening to spill tea all over her blazer as she carefully navigated between tables. Scanning the overcrowded room for a spare seat, she spotted a distinguished gentleman in a large corner booth sitting alone.

"That booth can seat an army," Leah muttered to herself. "I wonder if he would mind a little company today?" she thought wistfully as she bumped into another chair.

Leah surveyed the room one more time and decided to sidle over to his corner. Desperate for a change of venue in order to tackle a contentious corporate memo, she would do anything for a seat in her favorite café. She paused against the wall just behind his left shoulder and surveyed the scene.

On his table, there was a small pot of tea placed within reach of a fine porcelain cup and saucer. The gentleman was engrossed in a worn, leather-bound book. The large knuckles in his left hand held the pages open while his weathered right hand gingerly held the handle of his tea cup. His tweed jacket and wool scarf hung from a hook on the wall next to Leah and smelled of pipe and leather and the musty, friendly scent of stories untold. His posture suggested a life-time of discipline, while the slight curve of his shoulders hinted of burdens unavoidable by time. There was a reverence in his breath and a quiet approachability about him.

Spotting a cramped alcove table adjacent to the gentleman, Leah carefully balanced her tea, scone, and laptop as she slid into the limited space. She struggled to remove her coat and reached for her cup. Taking the first sip, Leah flinched noticeably as the scalding tea touched her lips. The cup clattered into the saucer as Leah sucked in a giant gulp of air and exhaled with frustration.

"Hot!" she exclaimed under her breath.

The gentleman glanced up from his book. His eyebrows slightly arched toward the frazzled young lady with her back to him.

Leah abruptly pushed the drink away and opened her laptop. Her mood intensified as she surveyed the blinking cursor on her blank screen. Paralyzed by the thought of the myriad lives that would be impacted by her words, she felt a tightness in her chest. Her heart rate seemed to escalate the pulse of the hypnotic cursor, mocking her more aggressively with each second that passed.

"I think I may have just scalded my brain, too," Leah thought, impatiently willing some inspiration while tapping her fingers on the table.

An unfamiliar voice broke the silence.

"What story are you writing?" His tone was gruff, but inviting. It offered to soothe her frustration like a warm cup of tea.

Without turning, Leah responded with a hopeless exhale accompanied by the words, "No story—just an email."

He paused.

"Sounds important." His voice was both thoughtful and firm. Too firm for Leah.

"It is," Leah responded impatiently, hoping to dismiss the uninvited onlooker.

"Hmm. Then it should be a good *story*."

Something about his thoughtfulness irritated Leah. The scalding tension plaguing her thoughts hit a boiling point and she spun in her seat to face her intrusive neighbor. "It's *not* a story—it's an *email* to my team. But you are correct—it *is* very important. I need to get the words right because what I have to tell them could impact each of their jobs—maybe even the entire company. In fact, that's why I came here today—to find some space and *quiet* to focus on the task at hand." Leah managed a terse smile, while meeting his gaze. She deliberately reached for her scone and took a defiant bite, chewing to the beat of her elevated heart rate.

Her eyes met the steady gaze of her onlooker, who studied her with intention. He immediately noticed a few stray crumbs slip down Leah's chin, and a grin slowly spread from behind his thick gray beard. His bright sapphire eyes sparkled, accented by the dark blue, round-rimmed glasses that framed a perfectly shaved head.

"So you need to motivate your team to do something important to save the day, and if they don't, all is lost?" His words posed a small challenge while he held her gaze with compassion and understanding.

Leah dropped her eyes in resignation, hoping to end the conversation. She self-consciously wiped the crumbs off her chin.

"Well, you are right about that. I do need them to do something that will set a new precedent in our company, and at the risk of sounding dramatic, I've been told that the whole organi-zation could go under if my efforts are unsuc-cessful. Now, if you will excuse me, I really need to finish this email." Leah spun around in her seat to face the nagging blinking cursor, which at least didn't talk back.

"Sounds exciting—just like a good story," the gentleman persisted, his voice trailing off. Leah rolled her eyes and turned slowly to make one last comment, only to discover he had disappeared.

"Finally," she said to herself, and she spun back to her laptop.

The server stopped by Leah's table to clear the dish that once held her blueberry scone.

"Some talkative people here today," Leah com-mented sarcastically.

"You must be talking about the Professor?" the server smiled. "He's here every morning before class and sometimes on Saturdays. He teaches at the university." She turned to wipe the table next to her. "He's not usually a big talker, so whatever he said had to be important."

Leah lifted her teacup to take a sip and realized just how long she had been sitting. The now-cold brew had lost all of its zip. Placing the porcelain cup back in the saucer, Leah shut her laptop in defeat. Even the quiet was too deafening today. As the newest manager at Blaise International, Leah felt added pressure to perform and prove herself in her role. For six years she hustled to earn the promotion, only to feel inadequate in the face of her first challenge.

Leah stuffed the laptop into her bag and dodged tables on her way to the large oak door—an icon of the old Brighton Tea Room. She paused on the steps of the historic building, surveying several tranquil couples on a Saturday morning stroll.

"Oh, to be carefree today, with nothing on my mind," Leah sighed as she slung her bag over her shoulder. She turned and walked toward her apartment, a new complex just beyond the university campus.

The shortest route home involved cutting through the tree-lined, ivy-covered campus. School would commence in a few weeks, so today was remarkability still—just scattered faculty and staff moving about in their electric carts, making last-minute preparations for the onslaught of new and returning students.

Leah fixed her gaze on her feet, strolling thoughtfully through the campus, while contemplating the email she was putting off. Her hands were shoved deep in her coat pockets while her thoughts kept time with her casual cadence.

"Finish your story?"

She was startled out of her trance by the voice coming from a bench nestled under a cluster of old oak trees. Pausing to fully absorb the moment, Leah pivoted to catch her first glimpse of the Professor sitting in the shade of the old oak tree, reading a book.

"*Not* a story, just an email," she said deliberately, with a hint of exhaustion in her voice. The Professor closed his book and rested it on his lap.

"You will be hard-pressed to motivate those you lead with just an email." His tone was reassuring. "People need a reason to move— they need a story."

"I understand you are a professor at the university?" Leah attempted to change the subject.

"Thirty-five years this semester."

"What do you teach?" Leah felt suddenly curious to better understand this mysterious man.

"I teach leadership courses to empower people to achieve impossible results in order to save their jobs and possibly their companies," the Professor teased.

Leah's face softened into a wry grin. "Sounds like a daunting class."

"I assure you, it is not as daunting as you might think. Actually, it's fairly simple, if you are willing to change your perspective."

"I have a new, demanding role at work and really don't have time to take a class." Leah smiled politely.

"No worries," the Professor said as he slid down the bench. "Why don't you join me and tell me a little bit about your company." He motioned for Leah to take a seat next to him.

Leah took a seat on the bench and rested her bag on her lap. After a momentary hesitation, she relaxed and began to speak while fixing her gaze on the horizon.

"My company has been around for nearly 40 years, manufacturing products that help people in their everyday lives. Over the last several years, we have seen increased competition with our core product lines, causing us to shift our focus to our innovation team to develop new products. Recently, we introduced one of the team's new products to the market. The product has the ability to save our customers money while increasing their productivity. We trained the entire sales team, yet our sales are slow—nonexistent really—and the lackluster sales orders have placed us in a precarious position. If we can't improve sales in the next quarter, I will have to begin laying people off—something we haven't done since the company began."

The Professor reached into his coat pocket and removed a small notebook and a fountain pen. He rustled through a few pages and started to scribble a few notes. Leah paused and looked down at his writing.

"Been awhile since I've actually handled a pen," Leah commented wryly.

Folding his notebook over his pen, he smiled at Leah. "For me, putting pen to paper changes my perspective and sparks creativity," he said thoughtfully. "You are facing a challenge that will require a creative solution. Years of study have taught me that people are hardwired for story. Thousands of years before email or memos, we relied on stories to communicate." He opened the notebook and pointed to his notes. "Story is the language of life. Each experience we have in life comes through some type of story. The story you just told me about your company is compelling and sounds like the perfect opening paragraph for an important email."

**PROFESSOR MAXIM:**

Story is the language of life. Each experience we have in life comes through some type of story.

Leah let his words soak in. She was curious why he was talking so much about "story" when she had a business challenge; however, her mind began to contemplate a new range of ideas. Unbuckling her bag, she extracted her laptop to take a few notes.

"Everyone in our company knows this story. Why would this be the opening paragraph to my email?" Leah's curiosity was piqued by the sudden inspiration.

"Great question," the Professor replied. "Let me give you a helpful maxim to remember — never assume everyone knows what you know at the level you know." He paused for effect. "Since everyone experiences stories differently, the way people think and feel about any topic can be different."

Leah's fingers were flying over the keyboard as she spoke, "So even though we have all experienced the same story, we can walk away with different ways of thinking and feeling about the story?"

"In a word, yes."

Leah stopped typing. "How do you explain that?"

"Another great question. We experience stories in three ways. Depending on how aligned these stories are, I can think and feel differently about any topic."

"Three ways to experience a story?" Leah asked.

"Yes, but maybe we should save that for next time." The Professor replaced the top to his fountain pen. "You have an email to write."

"More like a story," Leah smiled with relief.

The Professor grinned as he rose from the bench. "Human behavior is directly impacted by how they think and feel about a story. How, then, should they think and feel about your new product? Tell them that story and gauge their response."

---

**PROFESSOR MAXIM:**

Human behavior is directly impacted by how they think and feel about a story.

---

The Professor turned and began to walk toward the campus center.

"Thank you," Leah called after him.

Pausing, the Professor spun towards Leah. "It's my pleasure."

Leah rose, still holding her opened laptop. "I'm very sorry about earlier at the coffee house. I was a bit stressed and rude."

The Professor grinned. "It's understandable. No worries."

"My name is Leah."

"Leah, it's very nice to meet you. Enjoy writing your story."

"Can we talk again sometime?"

The Professor recognized the hope in Leah's voice. "I'll be having tea here next week at the same time. You are more than welcome to join me. I would really enjoy hearing how your story turns out." The Professor gave her a friendly wave and continued down the path.

Leah carefully sat back down on the bench and propped her laptop on her knees. Her mind was racing. Pulling up her email, she began to type the story she was certain her team needed to hear. Recalling the basics from a writing class she took in college, Leah made sure there was a protagonist, a conflict, and a pathway through to the resolution.

The words that had eluded her earlier now flowed onto the screen with ease. Moments later, she looked up and realized the message she had been agonizing over for days was finally articulated as a compelling story. But, would it be enough? She scanned her notes one last time to ensure she didn't forget any of the wisdom imparted by the Professor.

**LEAH'S NOTES FROM THE PROFESSOR:**

**1** We are all hardwired for story

**2** Story is the language of life—each experience we have in life comes through some type of story

**3** We experience stories in three ways. The alignment of these three stories determines the ultimate interpretation.

**4** Human behavior is directly impacted by how people think and feel about a story.

---

**A HELPFUL MAXIM TO REMEMBER:**

"Never assume everyone knows what you know at the level you know."

# The
# IN-PERSON
# STORY

"We are teaching always; if needed, use words."

The sun bounced off the sidewalk in front of the Brighton Tea Shop, lighting the glass on the old wood door. Leah squinted as she walked up the steps and pulled on the brass handle. Her laptop bag swiped the small brass bell, signaling her arrival. She paused for a moment as her eyes adjusted and moved toward the counter.

"Assam tea, please," she asked, while scanning the room for the Professor. "And can I get that to go?"

Leah gingerly picked up the steaming cup and within moments was back outside and en route to the bench just outside the quad-rangle of the old university. She traversed the well-manicured grounds of the 200-year-old campus and noticed the Professor sipping his tea while reading a book on his favorite bench.

"How did your story turn out?" he asked. without looking up.

Leah stopped in her tracks. "Great. Then not so great."

The Professor lowered his book and motioned for Leah to take a seat. "Well, let's start with what was great about your story."

"Well, the response from the team was amazing. Even the top leadership of the company commented on the email…I mean, the *story*."

"That sounds encouraging," the Professor smiled at her enthusiasm.

"It was. People were sharing stories and talking about the future. Honestly, it was one of the most rewarding weeks of my career. We even experienced a slight uptick in our sales pipeline, which is a leading indicator for future sales. Everything was going great... well, until..." Leah's voice trailed off.

"I am guessing this is where you share the not-so-great part?" the Professor prodded.

Leah nodded her head in silence.

"Let me guess. People began falling into old habits by the end of the week." The Professor leaned back casually and took a sip of his tea.

Leah was startled. "How did you know?"

"Do you remember the last time we spoke, I told you we experience a story in three ways?"

Leah nodded, already pulling out her laptop to take notes.

"The three ways we experience a story is when we show up, when we speak up, and when we sync up," the Professor spoke deliberately while counting on his fingers.

---

**PROFESSOR MAXIM:**

The three ways we experience a story is when we show up, when we speak up, and when we sync up

---

"What do you mean we experience a story when we show up?" Leah continued to take notes.

The Professor crossed his legs and took another sip of his tea. "You ask the best questions, Leah."

The words of affirmation drew out a warm smile from Leah.

We tell a non-verbal story each time we are in the presence of other people. Our non-verbal story informs the listener on matters at hand. We have been informally taught how to interpret others' non-verbal cues through our own life story. Since each of our life stories is different, our interpretation of others' non-verbal cues vary, at times wildly, which can create confusion. Confusion is the enemy of progress." The Professor sketched in his notebook as he spoke. "Take for example, if I were to show up late to class for multiple classes in a row. What might my students think and feel about me and the class I am teaching?"

"I had that experience in college," she blurted out, undaunted by his Socratic style. "I thought that professor never cared about our class. In fact, it was my worst grade that semester."

"Understandable. The story the teacher conveyed, without saying a word, was that he didn't care about you or the class," the Professor replied. "The challenge we face is that we may never know all the facts. Perhaps, for example, your teacher had to travel the entire distance of the campus to get from one class to another. This not only changes the story, it allows you to alter your personal perspective about his tardiness."

The Professor paused to take a long sip of tea. "The non-verbal story is always subject to the bias of the interpreter. Said another way— how a person thinks and feels becomes the lens through which they see the world."

Leah typed furiously to keep up with his words. She took a mental inventory of the previous week.

"I wonder if the presence of any leader in our company told a non-verbal story that contradicted what she had presented formally to the team?" she pondered.

"It's a valuable discipline to take periodic mental reviews of past behavior," the Professor commented. "The manner in which we show up is important to motivate people to keep doing what we need them to do. If the story expressed by our presence is not aligned with the story we tell out loud, we lose momentum."

"In multiple meetings last week, a couple of our key leaders not only showed up late, but also spent more time checking their phones than participating in the conversation," Leah acknowledged with frustration.

"And how does that make you think and feel now?"

"Like they don't give a darn about our situation."

"You may have missed that non-verbal cue the first time, but I can assure you that your team did not. Thus, the regression in momentum," the Professor said. "People will, for the most part, give others the benefit of the doubt, until they can no longer justify trusting them. When our behavior is consistently misaligned with what we say out loud, confusion derails momentum. Our internal default interprets the confusion using our current confirmation bias. We have no way of knowing why the leaders were late or why they were entangled in their phones unless they tell the team. A story left uninterpreted is vulnerable to be misinterpreted by others. Here is a maxim to remember: We are teaching always; if needed, use words."

---

**PROFESSOR MAXIM:**

A story left uninterpreted is vulnerable to be misinterpreted by others.

---

"How do I fix this?" she asked as she typed.

"Depends on what you are trying to fix," the Professor said with a clever smile.

"I need others to tell a better non-verbal story when they show up," Leah blurted as the Professor chuckled. "I mean, leaders need to *show up* when they *show up*," she said with a wry grin.

The Professor gathered his book and tea as he stood. "It seems you now understand an important part of your ongoing story. What do you think is essential in order to understand the full story?"

Leah stopped typing and pondered the question. "You mean, if leaders think and feel it's acceptable behavior to be late and work on their phones, they may not understand the story they are telling?"

The Professor smiled. "Something to consider." He turned to walk away. After a few steps, he spun around. "I am enjoying our talks. I have faith you will regain your momentum. See you next week, and we can discuss how to accelerate it?"

"Yes!" Leah smiled with enthusiasm. "Thank you!"

The Professor gave her a quick wave as he continued down the path.

Reviewing her notes, Leah realized they had only covered one of the three ways people experience a story. She typed a quick reminder to ask him about the other two next week. She added one additional thought to the bottom of the list: Spend time with other leaders, teaching them about the impact of non-verbal storytelling.

**LEAH'S NOTES FROM THE PROFESSOR:**

**1** The three ways we experience a story:

   **A** Show up

   **B** Speak up

   **C** Sync up

**2** We tell a non-verbal story each time we are in the presence of other people. That story, left uninterpreted, is vulnerable to misinterpretation.

**3** Confusion is the enemy of progress.

**4** Most people will default to giving the benefit of the doubt, but not everyone; it's best to check in to ensure others don't check out.

---

**A HELPFUL MAXIM TO REMEMBER:**

"We are teaching always; if needed, use words."

---

**LEAH'S NEW STORY:**

Evaluate the non-verbal story I want to tell when I show up.

**1** I want my team to think and feel that I'm fully engaged. I will do this by:

   **A** Greeting everyone by name

   **B** Actively listening before speaking

**2** I will notice the story others tell while with the team.

   **A** If the story is misaligned, I need to schedule time to provide insightful feedback and coaching.

   **B** If the team's non-verbal story is aligned, I need to provide recognition.

# The
# OUT-LOUD
# STORY

"How we say what we say is as important
as what we say."

Leah was balancing two cups of tea on her lap when the Professor appeared.

"The young lady at the tea shop informed me my tea would be waiting for me on my favorite bench."

"It was the least I could do given how much you have helped me," Leah said as she carefully handed him the steaming cup.

"Helped you, how?" the Professor asked, taking the cup while slowly lowering himself to the bench. The crisp fall air caused a faint cloud of steam to escape from his beverage.

"This week was somewhat intimidating, but certainly rewarding," Leah said thoughtfully.

"Intimidating how?"

"Well, I had conversations with key members of our leadership team and spent a lot of time instructing them about the importance of their story when they show up."

"And?" the Professor prompted.

"And, we all agreed that our non-verbal story needs to be aligned with one of our core values at the company: *Demonstrate Trust*," Leah explained. "We discussed tangible ways we can show up and commit to relaying our stories without assuming our team knows what we know."

"Outstanding follow through, Leah. That is a sign of exceptional leadership. Well done!"

As the Professor took an extended sip of his hot tea, Leah felt a warm rush of gratitude as she absorbed his compliment.

"Thank you."

"So, why was that so intimidating?"

"I had to address our leadership with new information regarding their abilities and behaviors. You never know how that discussion is going to be received," she replied.

"Really? Tell me why."

"When I joined the company, my manager at the time disclosed that she was ridiculed relentlessly for trying to present a leadership idea. That story has always stuck..." Leah hadn't even finished her sentence before she recognized the connection. "That was a story!" she exclaimed. "From six years ago!"

The Professor's smile beamed through his thick gray beard. "Yes indeed, Miss Leah. That was a story—a powerful story—told by a person of authority," he said.

Leah's laptop was open on her knees, ready for note taking. "We present our story each time we speak. Unintentionally, we often inform the way others think and feel about the matter at hand. We've learned over time, if a person hears the same story two to three times, they will begin to form a belief about that story. Our verbal storytelling is a powerful tool that can be misused, even weaponized, by some." His voice was steady, but firm. No longer too firm for Leah.

---

**PROFESSOR MAXIM:**

We've learned over time, if a person hears the same story two to three times, they will begin to form a belief about that story.

---

Leah continued to nod her head as she typed her notes. "So, you're basically stating that words matter."

"Yes, very much so," the Professor replied. "One of my former professors studied this idea. It is known as the *ideomotor effect*."

Leah sounded the word out loud like a kindergartner learning to read. The Professor smiled and continued, "Ideomotor is a big word to describe how the use of words prime how we think."

"So, this is used in marketing?" Leah asked.

"This IS marketing," the Professor said. "But don't forget, the tone we use when we tell a story is equally as important as the words.

Leah's face began to droop. "I'm recalling a time when I thanked a coworker in a snarky tone. I could tell it was offensive and unbelievable to him."

"What story do you think your coworker heard—the words of gratefulness or the tone of snarky-ness? A simple maxim to remember is: how we say what we say is as important as what we say."

"What about the email I sent? Didn't it have a tone?" Leah asked.

"True." The Professor reached into his pocket to extract his small notebook and fountain pen. Removing the top of his pen, he wrote quickly in his notebook.

He handed the journal to Leah. "Please read this to yourself, then out loud."

Leah took the tattered notebook and carefully read the sentence written in blue ink. "You are on fire!" Leah said out loud, somewhat quizzically. "I see what you mean, I read this to myself with a tone in my head. Now, hearing it out loud it could take on several meanings depending on the speaker and the audience."

"The story we speak has an impact on the way people think and feel, which in turn influences what they do," the Professor added. "Tonality isn't an exact science, but it is a great indicator. When in doubt, you should always check your tonality. Your verbal story is one way to accelerate change within your organization."

---

**PROFESSOR MAXIM:**

The story we speak has an impact on the way people think and feel, which in turn influences what they do.

---

"So, this is why you said it is important that what we say aligns with what we see people do?" Leah asked.

"Very good," he replied. "Confusion is a result of mixed messages."

"And confusion slows my team down," Leah added.

"Precisely," the Professor agreed. "Speaking of your team, what progress have you made in the last week?"

"Once all the leaders realized the impact of their non-verbal stories, we've been mindful of a more consistent message. As a result, some of my top performers have really begun to thrive."

"But you still have others that have not yet engaged?" the Professor asked as more of a statement than a question.

"Yes. I am getting pressure to let them go if they remain on the sidelines."

The Professor took a long sip of tea. "And what stories are they hearing—or not hearing—that is holding them back?" he asked thoughtfully.

Leah stared across the wide campus as though searching for an answer on the horizon. "I'm not sure. Do you think they are afraid to fail?" she asked tentatively, still staring off into the distance.

"Have people failed in the past?"

Leah's partial grimace was all the story the Professor needed. "So, the story they are not hearing has to do with failing?" she asked.

"When people are fearful of taking an inter-personal risk, it can be described as a lack of psychological safety," the Professor began. Leah's scrunched eyebrows invited the Professor to continue. "When people form a belief that speaking up is career-limiting, they naturally choose to remain quiet to avoid the risk. In a very real way, the story they are not hearing has disengaged them from an opportunity to achieve their very best."

Leah slowly nodded with understanding. "The new product we are launching will require our leadership team to approach the market in a very different way. Acting differently should always be preceded by thinking differently, and thinking differently requires a new story," Leah said as she typed on her laptop. "We need to begin telling stories that affirm it is okay to fail."

The Professor grinned at Leah's insight and then asked a probing question, "Are all failures equal?"

Leah stopped what she was doing to consider the question. After some thought she slowly answered, "Now that you made me think about it, I would have to say no." Leah stared at her laptop. "Failing to follow the law would not be okay," she added quickly. "But failing is necessary when trying new ideas," Leah said with a bit more confidence as she continued to debate the question out loud.

A grin appeared on the Professor's face as he jotted a note in his journal. "Very good, Leah. If there are different levels of failure, then having a clear story regarding what smart failure looks like would seem helpful," he prompted, placing his pen and notebook back in his pocket.

Taking his last sip of tea, the Professor shared a final thought for the morning. "You can accelerate your story when you provide recognition to others for living out the desired story."

Leah continued to type.

"Recognition of others is a powerful story," she said out loud.

The Professor stood slowly. "Very good, Miss Leah. One final question for you to consider this week: What is the difference between recognition and appreciation?" he turned to walk toward the center of campus. "I look forward to your answer when we meet next time."

**LEAH'S NOTES FROM THE PROFESSOR:**

1 The tone we use is just as important as the words we use.

2 Verbal story is one way to accelerate change within your organization.

3 Not all failure is equal—define a smart failure story.

4 Change is accelerated when you recognize others for demonstrating the desired story.

---

**A HELPFUL MAXIM TO REMEMBER:**

"How we say what we say is as important as how we say it."

---

**LEAH'S NEW STORY:**

1  I'm aware of my tone when I speak and the story it is telling.

2  Telling deliberate stories accelerates change. I will do this by:

A  Incorporating a brief story to support our purpose and results into existing meetings.

B  Linking what I write to our purpose, values, and outcomes.

C  Being aware of stories told in my presence that don't align with the outcomes we desire. I should correct these stories when they happen.

D  Using stories to coach others.

# The
# SYNC-UP
# STORY

"We live our story every day in what we do, say,
and repeat – personally and professionally."

Leah's leg bounced with nervous energy as she waited for the Professor. Sales were reflecting encouraging growth indicators, bringing new hope to her hard working team. The story was building momentum. By linking the story of their purpose to the story of their new product, they were experiencing the impactful correlation of effort and effect.

The Professor appeared, holding a small bag from the tea shop. "Today, let's celebrate your tremendous progress with a blueberry scone!" he announced cheerfully. Leah blushed with delight. "If I am not mistaken," the Professor continued, "it is your favorite."

"How did you know blueberry scones are my favorite?" she looked inside the bag the Professor handed her, astonished at his attention to detail.

"It was what you were eating the day we first met. It seemed logical that if someone were struggling to write such an important story, she would go with her favorite." The Professor took his seat next to Leah. "And I may have jotted an observant note in my journal." He winked playfully. "Writing something on paper often solidifies a story. You might try it sometime."

"I don't think I can even remember what my handwriting looks like," Leah chuckled while taking a peek in the bag. "Hey, there are two in here!"

"Well, if it is your favorite, I thought I should also give it a try. Who knows, it might become my favorite, too," he said as he took the first bite. Leah was touched by his kind acknowledgement.

"Thank you," she said softly.

"It's my pleasure, Leah," he responded as scone crumbs dusted his beard. "So, sales are on the rise? Your team is gaining momentum? What is one lesson you have learned in the last several weeks?"

Leah finished the last bite of her scone and pulled out her laptop to review her notes. "We can change the way they think and feel when we align the three stories, which energizes their engagement," she began.

"Excellent," the Professor replied. "You will notice that people will work hard for you because you are a good leader, but they work the hardest for a just cause that aligns with their purpose. When you connected the company's history of helping people to the new product, you bridged the purpose gap. Now, the company's purpose has become, in part, their purpose. Your just cause has become *their* just cause."

Leah was typing as fast as she could to record the Professor's words. Taking a deliberate drink of his tea, he frowned thoughtfully and asked, "What worries you the most about the future?"

Leah stopped typing to contemplate the question. "I wonder if we can keep this momentum—particularly when I cannot be there every moment to provide a pep talk," she replied as she stared across the manicured campus.

"Great observation," the Professor nodded. "Maintaining the story when you are not around requires you to align your internal processes, technology, and systems. I call this the 'sync up' story."

**PROFESSOR MAXIM:**

Maintaining the story when you are not around requires you to align your internal processes, technology, and systems.

Leah typed, while nodding in agreement. "Where do we begin?" she asked, clearly a bit overwhelmed.

The Professor smiled while brushing the last of the scone crumbs from his beard and shirt.

"Let me tell you a story," he began as he settled back against the bench and crossed his arms.

*A man approached three bricklayers one day as he walked to work. For weeks, the man had walked by their construction project. On this particular day, the man stopped to speak to the first bricklayer.*

*"What are you doing?" the man asked.*

*The first bricklayer looked up and in a sarcastic tone replied, "I'm building a wall, can't you tell? It's my job to lay bricks and build this wall."*

*"Very well," the man replied and went on his way.*

*He approached the second bricklayer. "What are you doing?" the man asked.*

*The second bricklayer looked up and quickly responded with enthusiasm in his voice, "I'm an apprentice learning how to build buildings out of bricks. One day I will become a master bricklayer and have other apprentices working for me as I teach them how to build buildings out of bricks."*

*"Very well," the man said as he continued on.*

*Coming to the third bricklayer, the man paused and asked, "What are you doing?"*

*The third bricklayer stopped what he was doing, and with a glowing countenance, he made eye contact with the man and replied, "I'm building a school for young people from around the globe to come learn from the wisest professors in the world. This wall will hold the stained glass, which will fill the room with a bright rainbow of colors, washing over students that will one day lead nations, cure diseases, and compose music to entertain millions. Yes, my kind sir, I am a builder of great people. That's what I am doing.'"*

Leah was enthralled, wondering if the Professor may have been the man in the story.

"There are three bricklayers in this story," the Professor continued. "All three were laying bricks, yet all three saw what they did differently. Tell me what you see in this story."

Leah closed her eyes as she recalled the story. "The first bricklayer was focused on just the job of being a bricklayer. For him it was toil and labor."

"Very insightful," the Professor commented. "For this bricklayer, his hands and feet were engaged to do the work. And the next brick-layer?" he asked.

"The next bricklayer focused on growing his career as a bricklayer. He sounded like an apprentice with the desire to become a master bricklayer," Leah answered.

"Excellent," the Professor replied. "He, too, was engaged with the hands and feet, but he also had his heart and mind engaged, as he was committed to teaching other bricklayers to build buildings."

Leah interrupted with confidence. "And the third bricklayer was all-in. For him, it was more than a job and more than a career. It was his calling—his purpose—to not only build buildings, but to also build students that would ultimately change the world!"

The Professor listened quietly, smiling as Leah continued, "He had his hands and feet and heart and mind engaged in a way that would do more than encourage other bricklayers. His story would encourage students and…" Leah's voice trailed off as she connected her next thoughts. "And teachers." The student here added shyly, "The man in your story is you, isn't it?" Leah peeked up to meet the Professor's eyes.

The Professor squinted and gave a subtle nod to confirm Leah's insight. "The power of a person living with purpose and telling that story in all he or she does and says, it can change the world," he said.

"You asked where you should begin in aligning your processes and systems," the Professor continued. "Begin with the processes and systems that connect, care, encourage, and reward people for living a life on purpose. When the story told by your internal processes aligns with the story you tell verbally or non-verbally when you're in the room, you will be able to create a sustainable environment for your momentum."

Leah was furiously taking notes on her computer.

"Pause for a moment and see if you can give me some examples," the Professor challenged.

Leah's fingers paused over the keyboard. "Regarding connecting, this would be an effective strategy to find and select our talent. It could also serve as a tool to connect our people to the correct teams internally."

"Absolutely," the Professor encouraged. "Anything else?"

"Internally, could this be how we coach, mentor, and exchange feedback with each other?" she asked hesitantly.

"Also true."

"We have very sound systems and processes designed to care for the safety, security, and wellbeing of our employees," Leah commented.

"It sounds like this is an area in which your company is excelling," the Professor acknowledged.

"Yes, it is. But now we need to ensure these processes and systems are completely aligned with our bigger story."

"How would you recognize a misalignment?" the Professor asked.

Leah thought for a moment. "If we say we care about our people, who in turn care for our customers, yet we neglect their physical, financial, and emotional wellbeing—our story may not be fully aligned. We should be developing the full person to support them realizing their full purpose," she said.

"Outstanding," the Professor said. "What's next?"

"Next would be encouragement," Leah answered. "We encourage people when we recognize them. This also tells a very powerful story," she said resolutely. "In fact, I believe this was the homework you gave me last week,"

"Interesting connection. And what did you discover?" the Professor asked.

"That you have been encouraging me all along," Leah began. "Through your active listening and feedback, you have also been consistently giving me recognition."

The Professor blushed as he continued to sip his tea.

"I reviewed all of the recognition we gave out over the last year. Sadly, most of it came from our top leaders at our big sales meeting this summer." The Professor stroked his beard as he contemplated Leah's statement.

"Why do you say, 'sadly?'" he pressed.

"I said 'sadly,' because this meant our recognition was infrequent and only top-down. That represents missed opportunities to acknowledge hard work, and it only recognizes a small part of what we do."

"That *is* sad," the Professor agreed.

"For the other areas of our business, when we do provide recognition, it seems we only recognize projects—particularly when people pull all-nighters to fulfill an order."

"Interesting," the Professor said. "Go on."

"It appears as if recognition is tied to projects that exemplify heroic, quantifiable results. Appreciation has been less about the person—including his or her character and the personal sacrifice that person may have made as part of a team." Leah's voice was serious.

"Very insightful," the Professor replied. "The right encouragement also connects the story to your empathy and care—all of which increase motivation. While we are all responsible for our own lives, I am reminded of a colleague of mine, Dr. Viktor Frankl, who once said, 'Life is meaningful, and the meaning of life is to help others find the meaning of theirs.' When we miss this important component of life, we ultimately miss much of life itself."

Leah nodded in agreement

"There is, however, one blind spot you should watch out for when it comes to recognition and appreciation," the Professor continued. "We tend to recognize and show appreciation to others the way we like to be recognized and appreciated. While there is nothing wrong with that, you should know that not everyone responds the same when it comes to expressions of recognition and appreciation."

Leah resumed her note-taking.

"And what about reward?" the Professor asked.

"Our rewards are quantified by the way we compensate people, along with the benefits we provide them," Leah began. "I now recognize the important story told by our offering of these rewards," she commented as she continued to type her notes.

"Rewards are often the forgotten heroes of storytelling," the Professor added. "Taking a step back to review the story your rewards are telling is a much-needed exercise. Continuous improvement teaches us to check and adjust our work to maintain our efficiency. The same thought should apply to processes and systems that connect, care, encourage, and reward our people." On that note, the Professor stood to leave.

Leah continued to type, hanging on his every word.

"In fact, the same idea applies to our personal relationships," he continued while standing.

Leah paused and looked quizzically at the Professor.

"In business," he explained, "These systems are called processes and policies. In our personal lives, we would consider these traditions and rituals." He watched Leah process the comment. "Every idea we have discussed applies to our other relationships," he continued with a smile. "I so enjoy our time together, Miss Leah. You are a tremendous leader."

"Thank you," she mouthed and returned his smile.

"Today, I deliberately didn't give you a maxim to remember. Your homework is to create your own maxim based on what you gleaned from our conversation today."

Then, the Professor turned to head back through campus.

**LEAH'S NOTES FROM THE PROFESSOR:**

1 When people have the right story, we can change the way they think and feel, which energizes their engagement.

2 You will notice people will work hard for you, but they work the hardest for a just cause that aligns with their purpose.

3 Begin with the processes and systems that **connect**, **care**, **encourage**, and **reward** people for living a life on purpose.

4 While we are all responsible for our own lives. Dr. Viktor Frankl once said, "Life is meaningful and the meaning of life is to help others find the meaning of theirs."

5 We tend to recognize and show appreciation to others the way we like to be recognized and appreciated.

---

**A HELPFUL MAXIM TO REMEMBER:**

"We live our story every day in what we do, say, and repeat – personally, and professionally."

---

**LEAH'S NEW STORY:**

1  I stay focused on the story I can control by reviewing my team's processes and systems to ensure they sync up with our bigger story.

2  I begin by **connecting** with the team in a meaningful way, which includes:

A  Learning about their purposes to inspire their stories to transform the job into a calling.

B  Helping them discover their strengths to better connect with those on the team.

C  Providing them feedback that is both insightful and helpful to their development.

3 **Caring** for my team is to care for their wellbeing. Which includes:

A Their development, both personally and professionally.

B Their physical wellbeing by walking and talking when possible. Movement creates energy.

C Their financial wellbeing, which means connecting them with our outstanding resources to better manage their finances.

D Their emotional wellbeing, by providing a psychologically safe environment.

4 **Encouraging** my team through recognition in public and appreciation in private by:

A Starting team meetings with deliberate recognition stories, which link back to our desired outcomes.

B   Learning the way my team receives
    appreciation so that I can show my
    appreciation on a regular basis through
    the appropriate story.

5   **Rewarding** my team with a thoughtful
    and comprehensive total rewards program.
    This includes:

A   Reviewing our compensation structure
    to ensure the story it communicates is
    aligned with our desired outcomes.

B   Checking and adjusting our benefits
    program to ensure the story is aligned
    with how we care for our people. If
    we say we care but our programs don't
    demonstrate it, we are misaligned.

# The
# BURNOUT STORY

"We face circumstances every day of life.
We choose our attitude and our focus as we
navigate through those circumstances."

"Why the down face today?" The Professor questioned as he gently lowered himself on to the bench. A delicate snow flirted in the air, providing a fine dusting for the picturesque campus. Leah sat quietly, staring at the fingers of steam floating effortlessly from her tea.

"Had to let someone on my team go today," she replied in a dull monotone.

"I'm sorry to hear that," the Professor replied kindly. "May I ask why?"

"Just wasn't submitting any finished work. Honestly, it seemed that he just gave up. It would take him forever to get anything done," Leah continued, still fixated on the steam. "The pressure from my direct supervisor to let him go was relentless," she sighed heavily.

"Well, there is nothing easy about that," the Professor said in a comforting tone. "I am curious," the Professor continued. "May I ask a few questions about the person who was terminated?" The Professor had already retrieved his pen and notebook.

"Sure. His name is Rudy," Leah offered.

"Did you, by any chance, notice Rudy being overly exhausted in the last several weeks?"

"Hmm. Now that you mention it, he had been dragging for a while. He was often late to work and distracted in meetings. In fact, he fell asleep in one presentation and began to snore," Leah reminisced.

"Did you also notice that he became increasingly more cynical about leadership, work, and possibly life in general?" the Professor asked as he made a few notes in his notebook.

"Yes," Leah said suspiciously. "Do you happen to know Rudy?" she asked while eyeing the Professor.

"I don't know Rudy, but I do know plenty of other people who have been suffering with the same behavior."

"Suffering?" Leah asked with curiosity.

"I can't be certain without speaking to Rudy directly, but it appears Rudy may be suffering from what some label 'burnout.'"

"Burnout?" Leah inquired.

"Possibly."

"How can you know?" Leah asked as she pulled her backpack closer to retrieve her laptop.

"Burnout happens when our personal story begins to encounter conflict," the Professor began. Glancing toward Leah, he noticed her bewildered look. "Our story comes into conflict when we begin to feel we are no longer supported by those who lead us," he explained. "Sometimes, our feelings about our lack of control are a direct result of insincere leadership, meaning unclear or confusing directions."

---

**PROFESSOR MAXIM:**

Burnout happens when our personal story begins to encounter conflict.

---

Leah stopped typing. "What do you mean, no longer supported?" Leah asked somewhat defensively.

"We've already covered that people need to feel a sense of purpose in what they do. We all need meaning in our lives—including the work-place. When we enter roles in life—husband, wife, teacher, doctor, or accountant—it matters. That is, until it doesn't matter any longer. When our meaning begins to fade away, we encounter 'burnout.' Extended periods of low psychological safety become a leading indicator for burnout since people don't have a sense of safety to express their thoughts," he continued.

Leah sucked in a deep breath of cold morning air and slowly exhaled, clearing her mind. "I can see where this relates to our story," she began. "Extended periods of exhaustion are our show up story," Leah typed as the Professor nodded silently in agreement. "The cynicism is our speak up story," she said before pausing and furrowing her brow.

"You are wondering about the sync-up story," the Professor said, anticipating her next question.

Leah nodded, then took a long, overdue sip of her tea.

"When people reach the last portion of burnout, they become ineffective in anything they do. Work that previously took them hours could take days or even weeks during burnout. They become out of sync with every process and technology because the stories no longer match. Normally, these people read every email as confirmation of the stories they are telling in their heads. For people out of sync, every email is accusatory, every process is broken, and all their personal systems no longer seem to work."

"Once someone gets to this point, is it hopeless?" Leah asked soberly.

"I choose to believe that nothing is hopeless, Miss Leah," the Professor said with a warm smile. "Understanding how burnout happens and the markers identifying it is the first step in prevention. Once it is identified, a person needs to be shown a way through."

"A way through? Don't you mean a way out?"

The Professor finished the last sip of his tea and leaned back on the bench. "Life is a series of varied, continuous circumstances. We can't get *out* of life, but we can navigate our way *through* life," he said reassuringly. "It is when our story seems to cease making progress that we begin down the path of burnout. Some might need a professional unpacker to help them unpack their circumstances and navigate to a new story. For most, there is one powerful strategy to maintain momentum through a burnout stage."

Leah stopped typing to take in the Professor's next words.

"When any circumstance arises in our lives, personally or professionally, we can choose the part of the story upon which we focus. We can choose to focus on what is outside of our control, *or* we can choose to focus on what is in our control," he said.

Leah resumed typing. "In every experience we create or encounter, we have the privilege of choosing our attitude and focus and determining what we can control or what we cannot control," she read back what she had just typed.

**PROFESSOR MAXIM:**

In every experience we create or encounter, we have the privilege of choosing our attitude and focus and determining what we can control or what we cannot control.

"Spot on," the Professor said. "For the leader, it is important to recognize the story you communicate to others. A misaligned story creates confusion about direction. This in turn creates additional work or even re-work while potentially lowering psychological safety. Since psychological safety is the pre-cursor to trust, the confusion will continue to spiral."

The Professor stood to dust the light layer of snow from his overcoat.

Leah blew the snow from her partially covered laptop as she gently closed it to place it in her bag. "I may have let Rudy go prematurely," Leah sighed.

"That is always a possibility," the Professor gently responded. "For Rudy, however, it is an opportunity to reset his story as he finds a way through. But that is *his* story." The Professor smiled and turned toward the campus. "Until our next tea," he waved cheerfully.

**LEAH'S NOTES FROM THE PROFESSOR:**

**1** The markers of burnout:

    **A** When we show up, we are exhausted for extended periods of time.

    **B** When we speak up, our stories are more cynical than normal.

    **C** When we sync up with our processes and technology, we are less effective because we are focused upon what is outside our control.

**2** The gateway to burnout is when we lose meaning in what we do.

---

**A HELPFUL MAXIM TO REMEMBER:**

"We face circumstances every day. We navigate our circumstances by choosing our attitude— becoming either a victim or a victor by the power of our own choice."

---

**LEAH'S NEW STORY:**

1  If someone on my team becomes unproductive, first evaluate the signs of burnout.

2  Create awareness around the markers of burnout by connecting beneath the surface level with my team.

3  Activity: Actively listen to members of the team to ensure they stay focused on what they can control.

4  Monitor my personal burnout level with those closest to me. In my recovery plan, I purpose to:

A **Retreat**

   i.  Manage my day so I can get 6-7 hours of sleep. Taking time away from my daily routine to let my mind, body, and soul rest.

ii.  Set aside short periods, 24-48 hours, of electronic free time to allow my mind, body, and soul time to rest. Spend this time connecting with those who care about me.

## B  Reflect

i.  Spend brief periods of my day reflecting on the messages that fill me and the moments that inspire me.

## C  Refill

i.  Gratefulness leads to generosity, which is the most effective way to rejuvenate purpose in my life. When I sense burnout, I will focus on what I can control, followed by gratitude and generosity toward others. If that doesn't work, I will find a professional unpacker to help me navigate my journey.

# The
# FOUR
# CULPRITS

"When there is an unintended outcome,
listen for the story of the four culprits."

Winter had arrived, and snow covered the grounds of the historic campus. Leah walked briskly toward the Brighton Tea Shop, anticipating the steamy cup of herbal goodness that would warm her up on this cold day. Leah entered the quaint café and quickly spotted the Professor sitting at his booth in the corner. His spot provided the perfect view out of a picture-framed window, which spanned the front of the little shop.

Leah eagerly approached him and noticed a cup of hot tea and a blueberry scone waiting for her. Her face, flushed from the brisk morning walk, radiated with pleasure. Sliding her backpack onto the floor, she took the seat directly across from the Professor.

"Thank you for meeting me today," Leah said before taking a careful sip of tea, pausing as it coursed through her chilled body.

"My pleasure, Miss Leah," the Professor smiled. "Your message was intriguing, so I am glad we were able to connect here given the early snow this year." The Professor noticed Leah struggling to articulate her thoughts. "One of the simple storytelling devices I teach my students is called High/Low. This helps the thoughts get moving and helps put words to daily circumstances. "

"That would be helpful today," Leah agreed, reaching for the scone.

"It's a really simple prompt," the Professor continued. "What has been the high part of your week and what has been the low part of your week?" he explained. "Our minds record these stories as they happen. We've learned, through studying how the mind works, that we tend to remember the highest of highs, lowest of lows, and the most recent moment. Unfortunately, we can miss so many important moments if we haven't developed our minds to recognize meaningful stories as they happen." He took a long sip of tea, giving Leah adequate time to consider his words.

Leah had cleared a spot on the tiny table to make room for her laptop. Her hands froze over her digital diary when she noticed the Professor removing his faithful notebook and fountain pen from his bag.

"Is the High/Low a part of how you use your notebook?" Leah asked.

"That, and other important stories I may stumble upon," he replied. "So, Miss Leah, what has been your high and low this week?"

Leah stopped typing, gently closing the screen of her laptop to remove any barriers between her and the Professor. "The low definitely comes to mind first," she said with a sigh. "It looks like we might not achieve our plan."

"And your high?" the Professor pressed.

"Can there be a high if the low is *so* devastating?" she asked with resignation.

The Professor made a quick note in his journal. "Our highs can usually be identified when we acknowledge for what we are most grateful."

"Well, then that's easy." Leah's face showed the slightest hint of a smile. "The high would be our time together, talking about how to build a better story," she responded. "But it seems the rest of my week was such a roller coaster of highs and lows."

The Professor smiled. "That is normal. Most stories have what is called a *story arc*. The story arc is the journey our story takes along the path to resolution," he continued, "Let's talk about your story. You already suggested that your low is the possibility of not achieving the plan." He then paused to clarify, "I noticed you haven't missed your plan yet, but you are nervous you *might* not achieve the plan. Is that correct?"

---

### PROFESSOR MAXIM:

Most stories have what is called a *story arc*. The story arc is the journey our story takes along the path to resolution.

---

"Yes," Leah nodded slowly. "The possibility of missing the plan looks very real."

"Let's deal with the part of the story we can control," the Professor reassured her. "What would the story look like or sound like if you were on target with the plan?"

Leah gathered her thoughts. "As far as what it would *look* like, there would be more booked appointments and deals signed by the team. What it would *sound* like would be the team telling stories of our success. The stories would also include how our clients are benefiting by using our product."

"Excellent observation, Leah," the Professor began. "The current outcomes tell a story. When they are desirable outcomes, the story will sound like what you just described. When your outcomes are undesirable, there is a twist in the story. Let me illustrate by recounting a story called *The Four Culprits*," the Professor continued.

*A King once had four noble knights to protect his kingdom. They were brave and loyal to the King in every way. While the King had a plan to grow the kingdom, the enemy of the King wanted to destroy the kingdom and all within it.*

*The King's enemy sent four culprits to derail the King's plans in an effort to overthrow the kingdom. Only the culprits didn't come from outside the kingdom, they came from within.*

*One culprit, called Commitment, whispered a confusing story into the ear of one of the King's noble knights. The knight could remember what he was to do but could not remember why he needed to do it. Soon, the knight lost interest and was defeated.*

*The next culprit, called Capability, found one of the King's noble knights and cast a spell on him, causing him to lose his understanding of how to defend the kingdom. The knight knew what to do but could not understand how to do it. Soon, the knight was confronted in battle and was beaten.*

*The next culprit, called Control, captured the King's noble knight and held him in a magical box with no walls. He was told he could free himself if he could answer a simple riddle of the magical box. The noble knight was consumed by the box and was never able to see there was actually no box at all. Soon, the knight laid down his sword in defeat.*

*The final culprit, called Culture, sat next to the King's noble knight and began telling him stories of the way the kingdom used to be. He told one story after another, confirming that the old ways were the best. The noble knight began to feel a longing for the past and rose up against the King. Soon, the noble knight was defeated but only after great damage had been done within the kingdom.*

The Professor allowed his voice to trail off as he finished telling the story. He then opened his journal and carefully sketched out a box with four quadrants. Above the box he wrote, "The Four Culprits," and in each quadrant he wrote a single word: Commitment, Capability, Control, Culture.

"When the story of your outcomes doesn't match the story you desire, check these four culprits."

Leah opened her laptop to capture the Professor's notes.

The Professor continued, "A culprit is someone or something that defeats your efforts in achieving a desired outcome. If the Commitment culprit were present on your team, what would the story look or sound like?"

Leah paused from her typing and looked at the Professor. "Low commitment would be an indication of people unmotivated to go the extra mile. You would hear conflicting or confusing stories of the desired goals being told inside the team."

"Exactly," the Professor agreed. "Of the four culprits, Commitment and Capability share a common theme. In many teams, the enemy is the difference between *knowing* and *understanding*. Someone can *know* what to do, but if they don't *understand* the why, their commitment is low. We have spoken about this before, when we discussed the importance of your team investing in the purpose and priorities of the company."

Leah flipped back in her notes to make the connection.

"As leaders, we sometimes confuse knowing for commitment," the Professor continued. When commitment is frequently low, there is a lack of clarity in understanding. We tend to explain the *what* and *when* but tend to leave off the *why*. The *why* connects to our purpose, just cause, and our desired outcomes, which is a critical part of the story. When we don't understand the *why*, commitment is low."

Leah continued to type as she looked at the Professor. "You said Commitment and Capability shared a common theme?"

The Professor nodded as he sipped his tea. "Yes, they do. Knowledge versus understanding has a direct impact on capability. Commitment is about our internal motivation, which comes from connecting to the *why*. Capability is about being able to do what is required to get the desired outcome." He watched Leah's hands fly across the keyboard.

"People can know what to do and yet not fully understand how to do it. When we confuse knowledge with actual capability, our outcomes suffer. At times, when someone's understanding is low, they will require additional development to get back on track," the Professor explained.

---

**PROFESSOR MAXIM:**

People can know what to do and yet not fully understand how to do it. When we confuse knowledge with actual capability, our outcomes suffer.

---

Leah stopped typing to ponder the Professor's words. The look on her face told a story, prompting his response.

"You look as though you just had an insightful moment," he said confidently.

Leah nodded slowly. "It would appear I'm the one who needs some additional development," she said with humility.

The Professor smiled as he made a simple note in his journal. Looking up, he offered a word of encouragement: "The leader who recognizes areas of personal development demonstrates a growth mindset. The growth mindset is an essential story for any leader. Without it, a leader will rarely realize the fullest potential from his or her team, and even more importantly, in his or her own life."

Leah smiled gratefully. "Tell me about the Control Culprit."

"Ah, yes," the Professor nodded. "The Control Culprit shows up when a person's internal narrative is focused on the parts of the bigger story, which are outside his or her control. With any circumstance in life, there is a choice to make as to how we will think and feel about our circumstances. We can choose to focus on what is within our control, or we can focus on what is outside our control."

"So, the Control Culprit shows up when we allow ourselves to be held hostage by some part of our circumstances that are outside our control?" she asked with growing confidence.

The Professor nodded as he picked up the rest of his scone. Before taking the last bite, he added, "The Control Culprit is the leading indicator of reduced accountability. On an individual level or as a team, when the story being told is focused on what is outside your control, accountability shifts and eliminates progress toward your desired outcome." The Professor chewed slowly on the remaining piece of his blueberry scone while Leah digested his words.

Leah paused to enjoy the remaining bites of her own scone with a few sips of tea.

The Professor picked up his fountain pen to make a note in his journal. Looking up at Leah, he said, "The last of the culprits is Culture."

Leah placed the tea cup gently on the table as she began to take notes. "How do you define culture?" she asked, still typing.

"Perfect question," the Professor began. "Culture, simply put, is the way people think, feel, and act. Our stories create the experiences, which then shape the culture. The stories we tell ourselves and others have the power to move people toward a desired outcome or freeze people in place by altering culture."

Leah looked up with curiosity. "So, if people make up the culture—and culture is the way people think, feel, and act—then culture is ultimately responsible for delivery outcomes?" The Professor nodded slowly, noticing the wheels turning inside Leah's head.

Leah continued, "That would explain so much. My team keeps slipping back into bad habits. It's as if they haven't heard anything we've talked about over the last several weeks."

The Professor smiled, pleased with her self-awareness. "If the way a person thinks and feels is challenged with a new story, they will most likely look to defend their story, not the new one," he said. "We've spoken on this before. We called it *confirmation bias*. Most people will look to confirm what they think and feel to be true, especially if they are not in a growth mindset." The Professor gently closed his notebook.

Noticing the Professor put the cap on his fountain pen, Leah knew her time with him was ending for the day.

"You are perfectly aligned as a team to realize the outcomes you are delivering today," he said gently, placing his pen upon the closed notebook. "If your outcomes need to change, then search for the part of the current story that needs to change. Culture is a sneaky culprit because most leaders tend to simply focus on how their people act. They forget about the stories they tell themselves and others, and how those stories shape how they think and feel."

The Professor stood to leave.

"Remember, Leah, how we think and feel drives how we act. Find the culprit that is derailing your progress, and change the story."

Leah slowly shut her laptop and smiled in appreciation.

"Our time together has been productive. Your leadership story is only beginning with many more chapters yet to write." The Professor smiled down at her. "Personally, I've enjoyed our talks while watching you grow each week." He slipped his pen into the breast pocket of his tweed jacket.

"There is certainly more for me to learn," Leah said, sensing the Professor was speaking with some measure of finality.

The Professor gave Leah a warm look of comfort. "Yes, Miss Leah, there is much for all of us to learn. But for now, grow with the information you have."

Leah stood to thank the Professor. "Our time together has been so very meaningful. I am truly grateful for you. I would say this is definitely my high for the week—and all the past weeks that we have met together," she said as her eyes began to moisten.

The Professor smiled warmly, tucked his tattered notebook under his arm, and placed his hand on her shoulder. "I look forward to our next cup of tea."

He walked across the café, pulled the century-old door open, and paused and looked back at Leah. "The good news, Miss Leah, is the power of our stories can change, well, everything." With a final grin, the old Professor disappeared into the city.

---

**PROFESSOR MAXIM:**

The power of our stories can change everything.

---

Leah stood frozen in place, taking in the Professor's last words. Something inside her whispered that those words would be the last she would share with him in person. Returning to her laptop, she finalized her notes from the morning.

**LEAH'S NOTES FROM THE PROFESSOR:**

**1** The Four Culprits of desired outcomes:

   **A** Commitment

   **B** Capability

   **C** Control

   **D** Culture

**2** The unseen enemy of a team is the disconnect between knowing and understanding:

   **A** People can **know** *what* to do and yet not fully **understand** *how* to do it.

   **B** People can **know** *what* to do and yet not fully **understand** the *why*.

**3** The leader who recognizes areas of personal development demonstrates a growth mindset.

**4** With any circumstance in life there comes a choice to make as to how we will think and feel about our circumstance. We can choose to focus on what is within our control or we can focus on what is outside our control.

---

**A HELPFUL MAXIM TO REMEMBER:**

"When there is an unmet result, listen for the story of the four culprits."

---

**LEAH'S NEW STORY:**

1   In the areas of the business where we are not delivering our desired outcomes, I will examine which of the Four Culprits is at work.

2   By checking the Commitment Culprit, I gain insight into the alignment of my team by reviewing how well they know our desired outcomes and their understanding of how they contribute to the outcome's success.

3   When I assume the team is capable of delivery on our outcomes, I allow the Capability Culprit to derail our long-term success. I must verify alignment on what needs to be done *and* the level of the team's capability to deliver our desired outcomes.

4   When my team brings me excuses, even if they are legitimate reasons, listen for what is outside their control. By refocusing the team on the correct story, the one they can control, we avoid getting stuck under the Control Culprit.

5   The Culture Culprit shows up when we fail to tell consistent stories around our purpose and values. By not paying attention to the way my team thinks and feels, I give the Culture Culprit an opening to derail the team. The experience I create when I show up, speak up, and sync-up needs to be aligned to prevent confusion.

# The
# EPILOGUE

"I've learned in life that in work, play,
or relationships, we are designed
to connect with others."

The bespectacled, ruddy-faced young man sat staring at the blinking cursor on the screen. He desperately searched for the right words as his fingers remained frozen over the keyboard. He reached to take a sip of his steaming cup of tea.

"Hot!" he exclaimed with impatience as he dropped the cup back into the saucer. "Figures," he grumbled as he turned back toward his screen.

"Writing a story?" a deliberate voice spoke from above him. Looking up, the young man's eyes met the kind smile of the sun-drenched figure speaking to him. Short, cropped, silver hair perfectly framed the face of the distinguished lady who was carefully balancing a blueberry scone in one hand and a cup of hot tea in the other.

"I once knew a writer and storyteller who sat in this same spot," she said as she took a seat across the table. "What story are you trying to write?" she asked as she poured her hot tea into the saucer.

The young man surveyed her with curiosity and then slumped back into the antique chair. He let out a heavy sigh of defeat. "An email to the girl I love," he said as his voice trailed off in resignation.

"Ah, matters of the heart," she smiled mischievously. "Now that is a noble story to tell. But, why the long face?"

His extended pause allowed the distinguished lady to sample the warm blueberry scone and take a satisfying sip of her tea.

"She doesn't know how I feel," the young man softly replied. "I feel like this whole relationship will crumble if this email is not perfect."

The lady placed her scone on her plate and shifted her weight slightly in her chair to make eye contact with the young man. "I've learned in life that in work, play, or relationships, we are designed to connect with others. How we do that determines how well we do this thing called life."

The young man gently nodded his head as he hung on every word.

"Would you like some help?" she asked in a tender tone. The young man's eyes brightened with a combination of suspicion and hope.

"How can you help me?"

The lady smiled gently as she pulled out her notebook and fountain pen. "My name is Leah. Let me tell you a story…"

# My
# APPRECIATIVE
# STORY

My first meaningful encounter with the art of storytelling occurred when my wife bought me a cassette Walkman—yes, a cassette tape. The first cassette I played wasn't music, but rather, a book on tape by Zig Ziglar, entitled *See You At The Top*. Immediately, my love of story began.

As someone who struggles with dyslexia, I was not a huge fan of reading in my youth. The discovery of books on tape changed everything for me. Today, decades later, I am writing the final section of my fifth book. To say that I am grateful for people such as Zig Ziglar and a multitude of others would be an understatement.

A few years ago, I was honored to hear the legendary advertising executive, Roy Spence, tell the story of his childhood. He recounted how he went to his English teacher mom to help explain the grade he received on an English paper. With 13 misspelled words, he still received a letter grade of A.

With all the love she could muster, she explained to Roy that it was simple—he was a terrible speller, but a tremendous storyteller. The words she chose next changed his life. She instructed Roy to not spend his time trying to be a better speller, but rather to spend all his time trying to become a better storyteller. And did he ever! I am appreciative for people like Roy Spence—who embraced the wisdom of focusing on his main gift—and were willing to tell their story.

What I've learned is that life is filled with these influencers—other people who impact our journey unbeknownst to them. Why is that important? In every role we play in life, each of us can be that person of influence to someone else—often to those we will never know or meet personally.

For me, it has been one of my greatest joys to influence the lives of my children through story. I appreciate their willingness to listen to me often and humor me when my stories sometimes faltered.

My appreciation would not be complete until I expressed my deep gratitude to my bride, Dee. We have embarked on our 30th year of writing our story together, each chapter better than the last. And we have learned to embrace each plot twist along the way to keep it interesting and full of joy.

When I speak of my family, it is only right to include my work family, given the amount of time we spend together. Over the years, my work family has grown as I have been blessed beyond measure with people in my life—too numerous to name—who have poured into me, and helped craft my story along the way. To each of them, I am deeply appreciative.

And finally, to the one reading these words, I appreciate you! It is a deep honor to play a small part in helping you build your story. My hope and prayer for you is that you find your voice in your unique story and one day share it with someone else—maybe even over a Saturday morning tea with pen and journal in hand!

# The Resources

***Man's Search for Meaning***
   Viktor E. Frankl (Author)
   William J. Winslade (Afterword)
   Harold S. Kushner (Foreword)

***The Fearless Organization: Creating Psychological Safety in the Workplace for Learning, Innovation, and Growth***
   Amy C. Edmondson

***Wired for Story: The Writer's Guide to Using Brain Science to Hook Readers from the Very First Sentence***
   Lisa Cron

***The Power of Moments: Why Certain Experiences Have Extraordinary Impact Kindle Edition***
   Chip Heath (Author)
   Dan Heath (Author)

***Thinking, Fast and Slow***
   Daniel Kahneman

***Social: Why Our Brains Are Wired to Connect***
   Matthew D. Lieberman

# Tony Bridwell

 As an author, international speaker, consultant, and coach, Tony Bridwell has been making a difference at some of the world's largest organizations for the past 30 years. He is the author of *The Maker* series, former Chief People Officer of Brinker International, and Senior Partner with Partners in Leadership, an international consulting firm. Currently, Tony is the Chief People Officer for the global tax consulting firm, Ryan LLC.

Tony is a highly recognized thought leader in corporate culture, leadership development, and human resources, being named 2015 HR Executive of the Year by DallasHR (the local SHRM affiliate) and also receiving the 2015 Strategic Leadership Award from Strategic Excellence HR.

Tony has been a facilitator and featured speaker for audiences of several thousand people and has presented for multiple conferences and associations, including the CHRO Exchange, DallasHR (SHRM), the HRSouthwest Conference, APPO, and UNOS. Tony is also a member of SHRM and serves on the board of directors for Southwest Transplant Alliance.

When he is not spending time with his family, Tony turns his efforts toward mentoring a small group of young men, cycling, writing, and podcasting with his daughter, Alli. With three grown children and three dogs, Tony and his wife, Dee, have called the Dallas area home for almost 30 years.

Visit

TonyBridwell.com

# More from Tony Bridwell
## *The Maker Series*

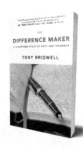   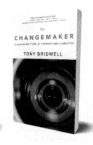

*The Difference Maker*
*The Kingmaker*
*The Newsmaker*
*The Changemaker*

Available on
**amazon**.com

BREAKFAST WITH SIS
A PODCAST ABOUT LIFE, LOVE, AND SWEET TEA

Available on:

Download the High/Low App to record your
meaningful moments of each day

Available on: